The Ultimate

Tiger

Book for Kids

Jenny Kellett

BELLANOVA

MELBOURNE · SOFIA · BERLIN

ISBN: 978-619-264-015-6
Imprint: Bellanova Books

CONTENTS

Introduction 4

Tiger Subspecies 7

    Sumatran tiger 8

    Siberian tiger 11

    Bengal tiger 13

    South China tiger 16

    Malayan tiger 18

    Indochinese tiger 20

Tiger Facts 22

Tiger Quiz 80

Quiz Answers 85

Word Search Puzzle 86

Sources 89

INTRODUCTION

The tiger is the largest cat species in the world. Famous for its beautiful orange and black striped fur, tigers have been an important part of many Asian cultures for centuries. The tiger is one of the 12 Chinese Zodiac signs and plays an important part in many Korean, Buddhist, and Hindu rituals and mythology.

There are hundreds of other reasons why tigers are adored by people like you all around the world. So let's learn more about them! Are you ready? *Let's go!*

Indochinese tiger.

TIGER
SUBSPECIES

Did you know that there are nine distinct subspecies of tigers? Sadly, three of these are already extinct. The living subspecies include the Bengal tiger, which is the most common, the Siberian tiger, which is the largest subspecies, and the Sumatran tiger, which is the smallest.

Each of these subspecies has unique physical characteristics and behaviours, so let's delve into each of them to learn more.

SUMATRAN TIGER

Panthera tigris sumatrae

The Sumatran tiger is a subspecies of tiger that is native to the Indonesian island of Sumatra. It is the smallest of all tiger subspecies and is characterised by closer-together stripes and a darker orange fur, which helps it blend into its tropical rainforest habitat. The Sumatran tiger also has a distinctive beard and mane.

According to the World Wildlife Fund (WWF), the Sumatran tiger population has decreased significantly in recent decades due to poaching, habitat loss, and conflict with humans. In the early 1970s, it is estimated

that there were around 1,000 Sumatran tigers in the wild. In 2008, the population was estimated to be between 300 and 500 individuals, and it is likely that the population has continued to decline since then.

Many Sumatran tigers live in protected areas, such as national parks, and are also protected by anti-poaching patrols by park rangers. In 2014, Indonesia's top religious body issued a fatwa, or religious decree, against poaching in an effort to raise awareness and protect these animals. As a result, killing a Sumatran tiger is not only against the law, but also goes against religious law in Indonesia, the world's largest Muslim country.

SIBERIAN TIGER

Panthera tigris altaica

The Siberian tiger or Amur tiger, is native to the Russian Far East, Northeast China, and the Korean Peninsula. It is the largest subspecies of tiger, with males weighing up to 300 kg (660 lb) and females weighing up to 136 kg (300 lb).

You can spot a Siberian tiger by their thick, long fur, which ranges in colour from orange to yellow and is marked with distinctive black stripes. They have powerful legs and large paws, which they use to move through the snow and capture their prey.

Like many other tiger subspecies, the Siberian tiger is endangered. There are estimated to be fewer than 500 individuals remaining in the wild. The main threats to the Siberian tiger include habitat loss, poaching, and conflict with humans.

BENGAL TIGER

Panthera tigris tigris

The Bengal tiger is native to the Indian subcontinent. It is considered one of the "charismatic megafaunas," meaning that it is an animal that is widely admired and has a strong presence in many societies' cultural and spiritual traditions.

Bengal tigers have been present in the Indian subcontinent for thousands of years, but today they are endangered.

There are estimated to be around 4,000 individuals remaining in the wild, making them the most common tiger in the world, but their numbers are decreasing due to threats such as habitat loss and poaching.

One of the most distinctive features of the Bengal tiger is its coat, which ranges in colour from yellow to light orange and is marked with dark brown to black stripes. The belly and the interior parts of the limbs are white, and the tail is orange with black rings. These unique markings help the tiger to blend in with its forested habitat and sneak up on its prey.

SOUTH CHINA TIGER

Panthera tigris amoyensis

The South China tiger used to live in parts of China. Sadly, it has not been seen for a long time and is thought to be extinct in the wild, however, many still exist in zoos across China and the world. The South China tiger is smaller than other tigers that live in mainland Asia, but bigger than the Sumatran tiger.

Males are about 3 m (10 ft) long and weigh about 130-175 kg (287-386 lb). Females are smaller, measuring about 2.1 m (7ft) long and weighing about 99-115 kg (220 to 254 lb).

A South China tiger at Shanghai Zoo.

Copyright: J. Patrick Fischer

The South China tiger has a lighter, more yellowish coat with narrow, sharp stripes. Its face, paws, and stomach are more white in colour. The South China tiger's habitat was destroyed, and there was not enough food for it to eat, which is why it is thought to have gone extinct in the wild. Fortunately, conservationists have had quite good success breeding them in captivity.

MALAYAN TIGER

Panthera tigris jacksoni

The Malayan tiger lives in the southern and central parts of the Malay Peninsula and in southern Thailand. It is the national symbol of Malaysia, and it was only recognised as a separate subspecies of tiger in 2004. Before that, it was thought to be the same as the Indochinese tiger. The Malayan tiger has orange fur with thin black stripes, which helps it blend into its surroundings when stalking prey or hiding.

Sadly, there are only a few hundred Malayan tigers left in the wild, and their numbers are decreasing due to habitat loss, poaching, and hunting for their body parts.

INDOCHINESE TIGER
Panthera tigris corbetti

The Indochinese tiger is native to Southeast Asia and used to live in Cambodia, China, Laos, Myanmar, Thailand, and Vietnam. Now, only about 250 Indochinese tigers are left, and they are only found in Myanmar and Thailand. These tigers are in danger of disappearing and are listed as endangered on the IUCN Red List of Threatened Species. Some people think they should be listed as critically endangered, which is the most serious type of danger.

Indochinese tigers are generally smaller than other subspecies, like the Bengal tiger. They also have shorter, darker fur with narrower stripes, which helps them stay cool in the hot tropical forests and blend in with their surroundings. Male Indochinese tigers have a ridge on top of their head that runs from front to back.

TIGER FACTS

Tigers are the largest cat species in the world. They are also the third largest carnivore on land, behind polar and brown bears.

• • •

There are nine subspecies of tigers, three of which are extinct: the Bali tiger, the Javan tiger, and the Caspian tiger.

A Siberian tiger.

Credit: Unsplash/Max van den Oetelaar

The largest subspecies of tigers is the Siberian tiger. An adult male can weigh up to 300 kg (660 lbs).

. . .

The smallest subspecies of tiger is the Sumatran tiger. An adult male weighs between 100 to 140 kg (220 to 310 lbs).

. . .

Tigers don't only have striped fur — their skin is striped, too. They are the only truly striped cats.

. . .

No two tigers have the same stripes, and the stripes are not symmetrical on both sides of their bodies.

The stripes on a Sumatran tiger (*above*) are closer together than on any of the other species.

Tigers have tails that are about three feet long; they help them to stay balanced when taking tight corners.

• • •

Wild tigers have a lifespan of around 10-15 years. They generally live longer in captivity (around 16-18 years). The oldest living tiger on record was 26 years old.

• • •

Tiger cubs stay with their mums for around two years before leaving their home range to start on their own.

A tigress and her cub at a zoo in Germany.
Credit: Waldemar Brandt

Tigers aren't fully grown until the age of five.

. . .

Tigers mostly hunt at night and alone. However, if an opportunity arises in the daytime to get a meal, they won't ignore it!

. . .

Tigers are fast! They can reach speeds of 49-65 km/h (30-40 m/ph). However, they can only maintain this speed for short distances.

Only one in 20 hunts end in a successful kill.

. . .

When tigers hunt, they usually attack their prey's throats while holding them down.

. . .

Tigers often take their kills to a safe place and bury them under vegetation.

. . .

Tigers can go for two weeks without eating. But when they do eat, they consume up to 34 kg (75 lb) of meat at one time.

Leopards, which are much smaller, hunt at different times of the day to tigers to avoid competition.

• • •

The gestation period (length of pregnancy) of a tiger is just under 3 months. They usually give birth to two or three cubs.

• • •

When cubs are born, they are completely blind and helpless. Their mums take care of them for two years, until they are strong enough to fend for themselves.

A Bengal tiger in India.

Unlike most cats, tigers are very good swimmers. You can often see them crossing rivers and lakes. They also enjoy playing in the water to stay cool on hot days.

• • •

Tigers don't live in prides as lions do. They mostly like to be on their own, but do establish home ranges that they stick to when roaming and hunting.

• • •

When tigers do form groups, they are called 'streaks'.

A close-up of a Siberian tiger.

Tigers have two types of roars: a 'true' roar and a 'coughing' roar. The true roar is longer, and the coughing roar is sharper and shorter, with their teeth exposed.

• • •

You can hear a tiger's 'true' roar from up to 3 km (1.9 mi) away.

• • •

Tigers' hind legs are longer than their front legs. This gives them the amazing ability to leap up to 10 m (33 ft).

Tigers have padded feet, which help them stay silent while stalking their prey.

• • •

The front paw pads of male tigers are usually larger than females, which helps other tigers know which gender they are when they spot tracks.

• • •

Tigers aren't too fussy about what they eat, but their favourite meals include antelope, deer, wild boar and buffalo.

A rare white tiger at a zoo in Colombia.

Tigers have white spots on the backs of their ears (**left**), which some scientists believe are used as fake eyes to scare off predators, which are behind them. Others believe they are used to help tiger cubs follow their mums in tall grass.

• • •

White, or albino, tigers exist. However, they are very rare. **(See photo on page 39).**

• • •

Tigers have round pupils, unlike domestic cats, which have slitted pupils. This is because domestic cats are nocturnal, whereas tigers are crepuscular (they are most active in the mornings and evenings).

Tigers wee, which they use to mark their territory, smells like buttered popcorn.

• • •

Tigers cannot purr. Instead, they squint or close their eyes to show they are happy.

• • •

One swipe from a tiger's front paw is enough to break a bear's skull or back.

• • •

Tigers have been listed as an endangered species since 1986 and we need to act fast to protect them.

A Sumatran tiger.

A Siberian tiger.

Female tigers are called tigresses.

• • •

The tiger is the national animal of Bangladesh, Malaysia, South Korea and India.

• • •

Less than 100 years ago, tigers lived in most parts of Asia, and could even be found in Turkey.

Shere Khan, the tiger in the movie *The Jungle Book* is a Bengal tiger.

• • •

Tigers have huge teeth. Their upper canines are around 10 cm (4 in) long!

• • •

Tigers are the most dangerous of the cats. They have killed more humans than lions or leopards. Although, it is not as common now as it was in the 19th century.

In rural India, some people wear masks on the back of their heads to prevent tiger attacks. This is because tigers usually attack from the side or behind.

• • •

If you look closely you'll see that Siberian tigers have fewer stripes than Bengal tigers.

• • •

The stripes of a Siberian tiger are brown, rather than black.

• • •

The South China tiger has the least amount of stripes.

There are almost as many tigers living in zoos and conservation parks as in the wild.

• • •

The print that a tiger's paw makes is called a 'pug mark'.

• • •

Tigers have such rough tongues that they can pull the skin off their prey with one lick.

• • •

All white tigers that are in zoos can be traced back to Mohan, a white tiger that was captured in India in 1951.

Tiger cubs playing in the water.

Credit: Frida Bredesen

Sadly, over the past 100 years, around 95% of wild tigers have disappeared. There are estimated to be only 5,000 left in the wild.

• • •

Sumatran tigers have webbed feet, which help them to swim.

• • •

The oldest tiger fossils that have been found date back two million years.

• • •

Tigers really love meat. In fact, they are called 'hypercarnivores', because their bodies can not digest any plants or fruit.

Tigers have individual scent glands, so every tiger has its own personal smell.

• • •

Tigers have the second largest brains of all carnivores, after the polar bear.

• • •

Domesticated cats share 95% of the same DNA as a tiger.

• • •

Tigers are very friendly when it comes to sharing food. While lions will fight over a kill, tigers take turns eating.

A tigress and cubs at Bandhavgarh National Park, India. *Credit: Syna Tiger Resort*

Tigers and the extinct sabre-toothed tiger are not closely related at all.

. . .

The Bali tiger was considered to be evil, so the local people hunted it to extinction.

. . .

Don't confuse Tasmanian tigers with big cats! They are actually marsupials, like koalas and kangaroos.

. . .

Tigers, like all other cats, can't taste anything that is sweet.

In Chinese medicine, it is believed that certain parts of the tiger's body can heal diseases. Sadly, this belief has led to much of the poaching that happens.

• • •

Tigers have great night vision. It is six times better than a human's.

• • •

A tiger's saliva is antiseptic, so they can use it to clean their wounds.

• • •

Like most cats, tigers love to sleep! They spend around 18 hours a day sleeping.

A female tiger preparing to attack in Bandhavgarh National Park, India. *Credit:*

Abhishek Singh

Around 60 years ago, there were over 4,000 South China tigers living in China. Now, they only exist in zoos.

• • •

Tigers are apex predators, meaning that they are at the top of the food chain and don't have many natural predators.

• • •

No one knows for sure where the name 'tiger' comes from, but many believe it originates from the Persian word '*tigra*', meaning pointed and sharp.

< **A Sumatran tiger**

Tigers are considered to be *'charismatic megafauna'*. This means that they are very popular around the world and are often used in campaigns by wildlife organisations.

Other species in this category include elephants, giant panda and the humpback whale. Sadly, this fame also means that they are commonly hunted by poachers.

• • •

The Caspian tiger was native to Turkey, northern Iran and other parts of Central Asia and western China. Sadly, it was officially named as extinct in 2003.

A white tiger in Singapore.

The Indochinese tiger
lives in Southeast Asia, in
Myanmar, Thailand and
Laos. The tiger is smaller
than the Bengal and
Siberian tigers, and it has
shorter, narrower stripes.

• • •

The tiger's closest
living relative is the
snow leopard.

• • •

Tigers have been
bred with lions and
tigers to make hybrid species: ligers and
tigons.

A tiger's tail is about half the length of its body.

• • •

A tiger's stripes aren't just beautiful — they are very important to help them camouflage in dense jungles and surprise their prey.

• • •

The tiger's prey are dichromats, meaning that when they look at the colour orange (like on a tiger) they actually see green.

Bandhavgarh National Park, India.

Credit: Sam Power

There are three colour variations in tigers: golden, white and stripeless snow white. However, white tigers are very rare in the wild.

· · ·

Tigers don't usually climb trees, but there have been sightings of them doing so.

· · ·

Adult tigers are solitary — but they are aware of other tigers in their territory, and aren't particularly territorial against them.

Male tigers will let female tigers and cubs eat from a kill before they do.

. . .

To mark their territory, male tigers will spray urine on trees. Both male and female lions will also scratch trees to let others know they were there.

. . .

Tigers have many different sounds and facial expressions. Although they don't purr, they make a sound called 'chuffing' if they are happy or in a friendly situation. This sounds like soft snorting.

Although tigers are nocturnal animals — they hunt at night — researchers put up secret cameras and filmed them also hunting during the day. This, however, only happens in areas where there are no humans.

• • •

Tigers mate all year round, but most cubs are born between March and June and in September.

• • •

When a tigress is ready to give birth, she will find a sheltered place such as tall grass or a rocky cave to help keep the cubs safe.

A Bengal tiger.

Tiger cubs open their eyes when they are six to 14 days old. At around two weeks their milk teeth start coming through.

• • •

When they are eight weeks old, cubs can start eating meat. It is at this time that their mother might move them to a new den.

• • •

Tiger cubs drink milk for five or six months, after which they will start joining their mothers on short walks and hunts.

Tiger cubs will stay with their mothers for around two years, but they continue growing until they are five years old.

• • •

A 2004 online poll by the television channel Animal Planet found that the tiger was the world's favourite animal.

• • •

The tiger is one of the 12 Chinese zodiac animals. It is depicted as an earth animal.

A Siberian tiger in the snow.

Tigers are carved into many Chinese tombs and monuments, as they are believed to ward off evil spirits.

• • •

Black tigers are very rare, but they do exist.

• • •

There are many famous tigers in popular culture. How many can you name? A few include Tony the Tiger (*Kellogg's Frosted Flakes*), Tigger, and Rajah (from the movie *Aladdin*).

The oldest living known tiger was Flavel, who was rescued from the circus and kept in a zoo in Tampa, Florida. He lived to the age of 25.

• • •

A tigress together with her cubs is called an 'ambush'.

• • •

Taiwan has banned the cross-breeding of tigers, and it is generally frowned upon worldwide, as many of the animals are born infertile.

A Sumatran tiger.

Tigers eat fish — if they can catch them!

. . .

Tigers have been known to imitate the sounds of bears to attract them and attack them. Bears are competition for tigers in some habitats.

. . .

Most tigers have yellow eyes, but white tigers often have blue eyes.

. . .

Tigers have great short term memories. In fact, they are 30 times better than humans!

The crossed marking on a tiger's head looks like the Chinese symbol for 'king'. This is partly why they hold such a high cultural status there.

• • •

The biggest threats to tiger populations are poaching, habitat loss and growing human populations.

• • •

Tigers are severely endangered. So what can you do to help? There are many organisations around the world that need tiger-lovers like you to help spread awareness. You can even adopt a tiger through the Worldwide Fund for Nature (WWF).

TIGER QUIZ

Now test your knowledge in our Tiger Quiz!
The answers can be found on page 85.

1 Tigers have better night vision than humans. True or false?

2 How old are tiger cubs when they start eating meat?

3 What is the tiger's closest living relative?

4 What is an apex predator?

5 How many hours a day do tigers spend sleeping?

6 Tasmanian tigers are a small subspecies of tiger. True or false?

7 What do Sumatran tigers have that helps them to swim?

8 What is the name of the white tiger from which all captive white tigers originated?

9 What do you call the mark that a tiger's paw makes?

10 Which species of tiger has the least stripes?

11 Tigers are the most dangerous of the big cats. True or false?

12 What does tiger wee smell like?

13 What do tigers have that helps them stay silent while stalking their prey?

14 What do you call a group of tigers?

15 How long do tigresses take care of their cubs before they set off on their own?

16 What is the gestation period of a tiger?

17 How many tiger hunts end in a kill?

18 What is the lifespan of a wild tiger?

19 What is the smallest subspecies of tiger?

20 How many subspecies of living tigers are there?

ANSWERS

1. True.

2. Eight weeks old.

3. The snow leopard.

4. An animal that is top of the food chain. Like the tiger!

5. Around 18 hours.

6. False.

7. Webbed feet.

8. Mohan.

9. A pug mark.

10. The South China tiger.

11. True.

12. Buttered popcorn!

13. Padded paws.

14. A streak.

15. Two years.

16. Just under three months.

17. One in 20.

18. Around 10-15 years.

19. Sumatran tiger.

20. Six.

Tiger

WORD SEARCH

```
F D S Z S U M A T R A N
C X Z A S T D S W F H H
M Z T I G E R H G F H K
A S S I B E R I A N Y P
L J Q W E B C X P B T I
A F U H G F I J H E E Y
Y G N N Q W E G C N S T
A F H Y G J H S C G F D
N D F S D L V W D A D G
J S N E R S E C S L T D
H P A N T H E R A H G A
N Z S D F H K T D S E D
```

Can you find all the words below in the word search puzzle on the left?

TIGER	SIBERIAN	BIG CAT
JUNGLE	PANTHERA	SUMATRAN
STRIPES	BENGAL	MALAYAN

SOLUTION

				S	U	M	A	T	R	A	N
				T							
M		T	I	G	E	R					
A		S	I	B	E	R	I	A	N		
L	J			B				P	B		
A		U				I			E		
Y			N				G		N	S	
A			G				C	G			
N				L				A			
				E				L	T		
	P	A	N	T	H	E	R	A			

SOURCES

Staff, L. (2010). Iconic Cats: All 9 Subspecies of Tigers. Retrieved 2 November 2020, from https://www.livescience.com/29822-tiger-subspecies-images.html

Siberian tiger. (2020). Retrieved 2 October 2020, from https://en.wikipedia.org/wiki/Siberian_tiger

Sumatran tiger. (2020). Retrieved 2 November 2020, from https://en.wikipedia.org/wiki/Sumatran_tiger

Facts, T. (2020). Tiger Facts. Retrieved 2 March 2020, from https://www.national-geographic.com.au/animals/tiger-facts.aspx

All About Tigers - Physical Characteristics | SeaWorld Parks & Entertainment. (2020). Retrieved 11 November 2020, from https://seaworld.org/animals/all-about/tiger/characteristics/

Sunquist, M. (2010). "What is a Tiger? Ecology and Behaviour". In R. Tilson; P. J. Nyhus (eds.). Tigers of the World: The Science, Politics and Conservation of Panthera tigris (Second ed.). London, Burlington: Academic Press. p. 19–34. ISBN 978-0-08-094751-8.

Novak, R. M.; Walker, E. P. (1999). "Panthera tigris (tiger)". Walker's Mammals of the World (6th ed.). Baltimore: Johns Hopkins University Press. pp. 825–828. ISBN 978-0-8018-5789-8.

"Sympatric Tiger and Leopard: How two big cats coexist in the same area". Archived from the original on 13 November 2020. Ecology.info

Sankhala, K. S. (1967). "Breeding behaviour of the tiger Panthera tigris in Rajasthan". International Zoo Yearbook. 7 (1): 133–147. doi:10.1111/j.1748-1090.1967.tb00354.x.

Sunquist, M.; Sunquist, F. (1991). "Tigers". In Seidensticker, J.; Lumpkin, S. (eds.). Great Cats. Fog City Press. pp. 97–98. ISBN 978-1-875137-90-9.

McDougal, Charles (1977). The Face of the Tiger. London: Rivington Books and André Deutsch. pp. 63–76.

Mazák, V. (1981). "Panthera tigris" (PDF). Mammalian Species. 152(152): 1–8. doi:10.2307/3504004. JSTOR 3504004. Archived from the original (PDF)on 9 March 2020.

Matthiessen, P.; Hornocker, M. (2008). Tigers In The Snow (reprint ed.). Paw Prints. ISBN 9781435296152.

Hayward, M. W.; Jędrzejewski, W.; Jędrzejewska, B. (2012). "Prey preferences of the tiger Panthera tigris". Journal of Zoology. 286 (3): 221–231. doi:10.1111/j.1469-7998.2011.00871.x.

Leyhausen, P. (1979). Cat behavior: the predatory and social behavior of domestic and wild cats. Berlin: Garland Publishing, Incorporated. p. 281. ISBN 9780824070175.

Robinson, R. (1969). "The white tigers of Rewa and gene homology in the Felidae". Genetica. 40 (1): 198–200. doi:10.1007/BF01787350. Brooke, C., & Brooke, C. (2013).

10 of the Most Interesting (and Unusual) Tiger Facts | Featured Creature. Retrieved 3 March 2020, from https://featuredcreature.com/10-of-the-most-interesting-and-unusual-tiger-facts/

AND THAT'S ALL, FOLKS!

As we reach the end of this fur-tastic journey, we hope you and your young explorer enjoyed every moment!

Your feedback means the world to us, and we kindly ask you to share your thoughts with a review on whichever platform you purchased this book.

Not only do your words bring us joy, but they also guide fellow readers in choosing the perfect book for their young adventurers.

Thank you for joining us on this adventure, and we can't wait to hear what you think!

Please also visit us at:

www.bellanovabooks.com

Here, you'll discover an incredible collection of engaging fact books, giveaways, and other delightful surprises for the whole family.

ALSO BY JENNY KELLETT

  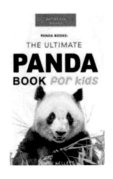

... AND MORE!

AVAILABLE IN ALL
MAJOR ONLINE BOOKSTORES AND
AT WWW.BELLANOVABOOKS.COM

Made in the USA
Monee, IL
12 November 2023

46381145R00057